WHERE ARE WE NOW?

Giorgio Agamben

WHERE ARE WE NOW?

The Epidemic as Politics

Translated by Valeria Dani

ROWMAN & LITTLEFIELD
Lanham • Boulder • New York • London

Credits and acknowledgments for material borrowed from other sources, and reproduced with permission, appear on the appropriate pages within the text.

Published by Rowman & Littlefield
An imprint of The Rowman & Littlefield Publishing Group, Inc.
4501 Forbes Boulevard, Suite 200, Lanham, Maryland 20706
www.rowman.com

6 Tinworth Street, London SE11 5AL, United Kingdom

First English-language edition published in Great Britain in 2021 by ERIS, an imprint of Urtext Ltd. This edition published by arrangement with ERIS © 2021 Giorgio Agamben. Translation Copyright © 2021 by Valeria Dani.

British Library Cataloguing in Publication Information Available

Library of Congress Cataloging-in-Publication Data Is Available
ISBN 978-1-5381-5759-6 (cloth: alk. paper)
ISBN 978-1-5381-5760-2 (pbk: alk. paper)
ISBN 978-1-5381-5761-9 (electronic)

♾™ The paper used in this publication meets the minimum requirements of American National Standard for Information Sciences—Permanence of Paper for Printed Library Materials, ANSI/NISO Z39.48-1992.

Contents

Foreword

The ship is sinking, and we are debating its cargo.
—JEROME, HIER. *EPIST.* 123.15.1[1]

This collection of texts was written during the state of exception that the ongoing health emergency has created. They are targeted interventions, sometimes very brief, that attempt to think through the ethical and political consequences of the so-called 'pandemic' and, at the same time, to define the transformation of political paradigms that the measures of exception have wrought.

Almost a year now into the emergency, we should consider the events we have witnessed within a broader historical perspective. If the powers that rule the world have decided to use this pandemic—and it's irrelevant whether it is real or simulated—as pretext for transforming top to bottom the paradigms of their governance, this means that those models were in progressive, unavoidable decline, and therefore in those powers' eyes no longer fit for purpose.

During the Crisis of the Third Century that unsettled the Roman Empire, Diocletian and Constantine launched a series of radical reforms of its administrative, military, and economic structures, instigating changes that would culminate in the Byzantine autocracy. In the same way, the dominant powers of today have decided to pitilessly abandon the paradigm of bourgeois democracy—with its rights, its parliaments, and its constitutions—and replace it with new apparatuses whose contours we can barely glimpse. In fact, these contours are probably not entirely clear even to those who are sketching them.

The defining feature, however, of this great transformation that they are attempting to impose is that the mechanism which renders it formally possible is not a new body of laws, but a state of exception—in other words, not an affirmation of, but the suspension of, constitutional guarantees. The transformation, in this light, presents similarities with what happened in Germany in 1933, when the new Chancellor Adolf Hitler, without formally abolishing the Weimar Constitution, declared a state of exception that lasted for twelve years and effectively invalidated the constitutional propositions that were ostensibly still in force. While in Nazi Germany it was necessary to deploy an explicitly totalitarian ideological apparatus in order to achieve this end, the transformation we are witnessing today operates through the introduction of a sanitation terror and a religion of health. What, in the tradition of bourgeois democracy, used to be the right to health became, seemingly without anyone noticing, a juridical-religious obligation that must be fulfilled at any cost. We have had ample opportunity to assess the extent of this cost, and we will keep assessing it, presumably, each time the government again considers it to be necessary.

We can use the term 'biosecurity' to describe the government apparatus that consists of this new religion of health, conjoined with the state power and its state of exception—an apparatus that is probably the most efficient of its kind that Western history has ever known. Experience has in fact shown that, once a threat to health is in place, people are willing to accept limitations on their freedom that they would never theretofore have considered enduring—not even during the two world wars, nor under totalitarian dictatorships. The state of exception, which has (for the moment) been extended until 31 January 2021, will be remembered as the most prolonged suspension of legality in Italian history—carried out entirely without objections from the citizenry or, significantly, from their institutions. After the example of China, Italy became the Western laboratory where experiments in new governing techniques were conducted in their most extreme forms. It is probable that when future historians make sense of what was really at stake in this pandemic, this period will appear as one of the most shameful moments in Italian history, and those who led and governed during it as reckless individuals lacking all ethical scruples.

If the juridical-political apparatus of the Great Transformation is the state of exception, and the religious apparatus is science, on the social plane this transformation relied for its efficacy upon digital technology which, as is now evident, works in harmony with the new structure of relationships known as 'social distancing'. Human relationships will have to happen, on every occasion and as much as possible, without physical presence. They will be relegated—much as was already happening—to digital devices that are becoming increasingly efficacious and pervasive. The new model of social relation is *connection*, and whoever is not connected tends to be excluded from relationships and condemned to marginalisation.

What accounts for the strength of the current transformation is also, as often happens, its weakness. The dissemination of the sanitation terror needed an acquiescent and undivided media to produce a consensus, something that will prove difficult to preserve. The medical religion, like every religion, has its heretics and dissenters, and respected voices coming from many different directions have contested the actuality and gravity of the epidemic—neither of which can be sustained indefinitely through the daily diffusion of numbers that lack scientific consistency. The first to realise this were probably the dominant powers, who would never have resorted to such extreme and inhuman apparatuses had they not been scared by the reality of their own erosion. For decades now, institutional powers have been suffering a gradual loss of legitimacy. These powers could mitigate this loss only through the constant evocation of states of emergency, and through the need for security and stability that this emergency creates. For how long, and according to which modalities, can the present state of exception be prolonged?

What is certain is that new forms of resistance will be necessary, and those who can still envision a politics to come should be unhesitatingly committed to them. The politics to come will not have the obsolete shape of bourgeois democracy, nor the form of the technological-sanitationist despotism that is replacing it.

ONE

The Invention of an Epidemic

Il Manifesto, 26 February 2020

As we face the frenetic, irrational, and unprovoked emergency measures adopted against a supposed epidemic, we should turn to the National Research Council (CNR). The CNR not only confirms that "an epidemic of SARS-CoV-2 is not present in Italy", but that, in any case,

> the infection, according to the epidemiological data available today for tens of thousands of cases, causes mild/moderate symptoms (a sort of influenza) in 80–90% of cases. Ten to fifteen per cent can develop pneumonia, but even then, the progress in most cases is benign. It is calculated that only four per cent of incidents need to be hospitalized in intensive care.

If this is the case, why do the media and the authorities go out of their way to cultivate a climate of panic, establishing a state of exception which imposes severe limitations on mobility and suspends the normal functioning of life and work?

Two clues might explain this disproportionate response. Firstly, we are dealing with a growing tendency to trigger a state of exception as the standard paradigm of governance. The legislative decree immediately approved by the government "for public health and security reasons" resulted in an actual militarisation

> of the municipalities and the areas where at least one person is positive and where the source of transmission is unknown, or in any instance where there is a case not ascribable to a person coming from an area already affected by the virus.

Such a vague and indeterminate formula will allow for the rapid diffusion of the state of exception to all regions, given that other cases are bound to occur elsewhere.

Let us look at the severe limitations on freedom levied by the decree:

- Prohibition on exiting the municipality or affected area for all individuals present there.
- Prohibition on accessing the municipality or affected area.
- Suspension of events or initiatives of any nature, and of any kind of assembly in a public or private space, even if of a cultural, recreational, athletic, or religious nature, and even if carried out in enclosed spaces open to the public.
- Suspension of childcare services and closure of every school, as well as suspension of attendance for academic activities and higher education, unless these educational activities are carried out remotely.

- Closure of museums and other cultural institutions and places listed in Article 101 of the Code of Cultural Heritage and Landscape (see the legislative decree no. 42 of 22 January 2004), as well as suspension of open and free admission to those institutions and places.
- Suspension of any educational trips on national or international territory.
- Suspension of open competitive exams and closure of state offices, except for the supply of essential services and for public utility.
- Application of quarantine measures, with active surveillance of individuals who have been in close contact with confirmed cases of the disease.

This disproportionate response to something the CNR considers to be a normal flu, not too dissimilar to the ones that recur every year, is absurd. We could argue that, once terrorism ceased to exist as a cause for measures of exception, the invention of an epidemic offers the ideal pretext for widening them beyond all known limits.

Secondly, and no less disquietingly, we have to consider the state of precarity and fear that has been in recent years systematically cultivated in people's minds—a state which has resulted in a natural propensity for mass panic, for which an epidemic offers the ideal pretext. We could say that a massive wave of fear caused by a microscopic parasite is traversing humanity, and that the world's rulers guide and orient it towards their own ends. Limitations on freedom are thus being willingly accepted, in a perverse and vicious cycle, in the name of a desire for security—a desire that has been generated by the same governments that are now intervening to satisfy it.

TWO

Contagion
11 March 2020

The anointer! Catch him! Catch him! Catch the anointer!

—ALESSANDRO MANZONI, *THE BETROTHED*

One of the most brutal consequences of the panic disseminated in Italy by every means possible during the so-called coronavirus epidemic is the idea of *contagion*, which forms the basis for the exceptional emergency measures enforced by the government. This idea, unknown to Hippocratic medicine, has its first, unwitting precursor during the pestilences that devastated several Italian cities between 1500 and 1600. This precursor is the figure of the anointer, or plague-spreader, immortalised by Manzoni in his novel *The Betrothed*, as well as in his essay *The History of the Column of Infamy*. A Milanese edict for the 1576 plague describes anointers as follows, and encourages citizens to report them:

> The governor has learned that some people with a feeble zeal for charity, in order to terrorize and scare the people and inhabitants of the city of Milan and to excite them to some turmoil, are applying ointments—which they consider pestiferous and contagious—to the doors and bolts

of houses, to the corners of the city quarters, and to other places around the state, with the intention of bringing the plague to private and public spaces. Many inconveniences arise from this behaviour, which has significantly affected the people of Milan (mainly those who are easily persuaded to believe such things). The governor hereby decrees that anyone, regardless of quality, status, rank, or condition, who reports within forty days of this announcement any person or persons who have favoured, helped, or known about such injury, will be awarded five hundred scudi...

Although there are some differences, the recent orders (issued by the government as decrees that we want to hope—alas, an illusion—will not be voted into law by parliament before they expire) transform, in effect, every individual into a potential plague-spreader, just as the orders against terrorism considered every citizen as a de facto and *de jure* potential terrorist. The analogy is so exact, that the potential plague-spreader who does not comply with the regulations is punished with imprisonment. Particularly frowned upon is the figure of the healthy or precocious carrier, who infects a multitude of individuals without affording them the possibility of defending themselves against him as they could have from the anointer.

Even sadder than the limitations on freedom implicit in these orders is, in my view, the deterioration of human relationships that they foster. Others, whoever they are—even loved ones—must not be approached or touched. Instead, we should establish between them and ourselves a distance that is one metre by some accounts, but that according to the latest suggestions by the so-called experts should be 4.5 metres (those fifty centimetres are so interesting!). Our neighbour has been abolished. It is possible, given the ethical inconsistency of our rulers, that whoever issued these orders did so under the same fear that they intend to instil in others.

Still, it is difficult not to notice that the situation which these orders create is exactly that which those who govern us have tried to actualise many times before: the closure of universities and schools once and for all, with lessons conducted only online; the cessation of gatherings and conversations on politics or culture; and the exchange of messages only digitally, so that wherever possible machines can replace any contact—any contagion—among human beings.

THREE

Clarifications
17 March 2020

In line with what is common practice in his profession, an Italian journalist has applied himself to twisting and falsifying my considerations on the ethical confusion—wherein not even the dead are respected—into which this epidemic has thrown the country. It is not worth bothering to name him, nor to rebut his predictable distortions. Whoever wishes to do so can read my text, "Contagion". Here I am instead publishing other thoughts which, regardless of how clear they are, will probably be falsified as well.

Fear is a bad adviser, but it is bringing to light many things that we have been pretending not to see. The first thing that the wave of panic which has paralysed the country showed, was that our society believes in nothing more than bare life. It is now obvious that Italians are ready to sacrifice practically everything—their life conditions, their social relationships, their work, even their friendships, as well as their religious and political convictions—when faced with the risk of getting sick (a risk that, for now at least, is statistically not even that serious). Bare life, and the fear of losing it, is not something that unites people: rather, it blinds and separates them. Fellow human beings, as in the plague described by Manzoni, are now seen only as potential anointers whom we must avoid at all cost, and from whom we should maintain a distance of at least one metre. The dead—*our* dead—have no right to a funeral, and it is unclear what happens to the bodies of the people we love. Our neighbour has been cancelled, and it is surprising that the churches are keeping quiet on this. What are human relationships becoming, in a country that has resigned itself to the idea of living like this for the foreseeable future? And what is a society that values nothing more than survival?

The other, equally disquieting, thing that the epidemic is making clear is that the state of exception which our governments have for quite some time accustomed us to has finally become the norm. More serious epidemics have happened in the past, but nobody ever dared declare for that reason a state of emergency which keeps us from moving, like the present one does. People have become so used to living in a state of perennial crisis and emergency that they seem not to realise that their lives have been reduced to a purely biological state. Life is losing not only its social and political dimensions, but also its human and affective ones. A society which exists in a constant state of emergency cannot be free. We live in a society that has sacrificed freedom 'for security reasons', and has hence condemned itself to living in a perpetual state of fear and insecurity.

It is not surprising, then, that when speaking of the virus one speaks of war. The emergency measures effectively force us to live under curfew conditions. But a war against an invisible enemy that can occupy any one of us is the most absurd of wars. It is, truly, a civil war. The enemy is not outside, but within.

It is not only—and not really—the present that is daunting, but the future as well. Wars have bequeathed us a great many nefarious technologies, from barbed wire to nuclear power plants. After the health emergency it is very likely that, along the same lines, governments will attempt to continue the experiments they could not previously complete. In schools, in universities, and in other public places, digital devices will replace physical presence, and the latter will be preemptively confined to the private sphere and to the enclosure of domestic walls. What is at stake is nothing less than the abolition of public space.

FOUR

Where Are We Now?

Commissioned and then rejected by
Corriere della Sera, 20 March 2020

What does it mean to live in the emergency situation in which we have found ourselves? It surely means staying at home, but also not succumbing to the panic that the authorities and the media are spreading every chance they get, and remembering that our neighbour is not just an anointer and a possible agent of contagion, but first of all our fellow to whom we owe our love and support. It surely means staying at home, but also staying lucid and asking ourselves whether the militarised emergency that has been declared in this country is not, among other things, a way of burdening citizens with the very serious responsibility that governments bear for having dismantled our healthcare system. It surely means staying at home, but also making one's voice heard and urging that public hospitals be restituted the resources of which they have been deprived, and reminding judges that the destruction of the national healthcare system is a crime infinitely more serious than leaving one's home without a self-certification form.

It means, ultimately, asking ourselves what we are going to do, how we are going to resume our lives when the emergency is over—because the country *does* need to come back to life, regardless of the far-from-unanimous opinions of virologists and of self-declared experts. One thing is certain: we cannot simply resume things as they were. We won't be able to pretend, as we have done so far, not to see the extreme situation into which the religion of money and the blindness of administration have plunged us. If the experience we have been through is to have any long-term value, we will need to relearn many things that we have forgotten. First, we will have to look differently at the earth on which we live and at the cities in which we dwell. We will have to ask ourselves if it makes sense, as they will surely tell us, to start buying again all the useless stuff that advertisers will try to force on us like before—or if perhaps it would be better if we could provide for ourselves at least some basic necessities, instead of relying on supermarkets for our every need. We will have to ask if it is still justifiable to fly for our holidays to remote places, or if maybe it is more urgent that we learn to dwell again in the spaces in which we live, that we look at them with eyes more attentive.

Among other things, we really have lost the ability to dwell. We accepted the transformation of our cities and villages into amusement parks for tourists, and now that the epidemic has made the tourists disappear and the cities that had renounced any other form of life are reduced to spectral non-places, we should be able to understand that these were wrong choices, as are almost all of the choices that the religion of money and the blindness of administrators suggest to us.

We will, in short, have to ask ourselves the only serious question that truly matters: not, as fake philosophers have been urging for centuries, 'where are we from?', or 'where are we going?' but, simply: 'where are we now?' This is the question we should be trying to answer, however we can and wherever we are. And it is a question we should answer not just with our words, but with our lives too.

FIVE

Reflections on the Plague
27 March 2020

The following reflections do not concern the epidemic itself but focus instead on what we can glean from human reactions to it. They are, in other words, thoughts on how easily an entire society surrendered to the feeling of its being plague-ridden and accepted self-isolation and the suspension of its normal life conditions: its work relations and friendships, its connections to loved ones and to its religious and political beliefs. Why hasn't there been, as would be quite imaginable and as usually occurs in these cases, opposition? My hypothesis is that the plague was somehow already present, even if only unconsciously, and that people's life conditions were such that a sudden sign could make them appear as they really were—which is to say, as no less intolerable than a plague. And this, in a way, is the only positive dimension that we can detect in the current situation: it may be possible that people will start wondering whether their way of life was right in the first place.

We should also seriously reflect on the need for religion that the situation has exposed. One sign of this need that has made itself apparent in the incessant media discourse is the terminology borrowed from the eschatological vocabulary. In order to describe the phenomenon, the media — especially the American press — obsessively resort to the word 'apocalypse', and often explicitly evoke the end of the world. It is as if the religious need that the Church is no longer able to satisfy is groping for a new habitat — finding it in what has already become, in effect, the religion of our time: science. Like any other religion, this faith can produce fear and superstition, or it can be at least used to disseminate them. Never before have we witnessed such a spectacle of divergent and contradictory opinions and prescriptions, typical of religions in times of crisis. These opinions range from the minoritarian heretical position (one that is nonetheless represented by distinguished scientists) that denies the seriousness of the phenomenon, to the orthodox dominant discourse that affirms this same seriousness and yet differs within itself, often radically, on the strategies for facing it. And, as always happens in these cases, some experts (or so-called experts) manage to gain the approval of the monarch, who, as in the times of the religious disputes that divided Christianity, sides with one current or the other according to his own interests, before subsequently imposing his measures.

Finally, another element to consider is the evident collapse of any commonly shared belief and faith. We might say that people no longer believe in anything, except in a bare biological existence which should be preserved at any cost. But only tyranny, only the monstrous

Leviathan with his drawn sword, can be built upon the fear of losing one's life.

For all these reasons, once the emergency—the plague—is declared over (if it ever is), I do not believe that it will be possible, at least for those who retain a modicum of lucidity, to return to our previous lives. And perhaps this is the most dispiriting thing we can see today—even if it is the case that, as has been said, "[o]nly for the sake of the hopeless ones have we been given hope"[2].

SIX

The State of Exception Has Become the Rule

Interview with Nicolas Truong for
Le Monde, 28 March 2020

In a text published by Il Manifesto, *you wrote that the Covid-19 pandemic was a 'supposed epidemic', nothing more than 'a normal flu'. Considering the number of victims and how fast the virus has spread—particularly in Italy—do you regret these statements?*

I am not a virologist or a doctor, and in the article in question I was only quoting opinions expressed by the National Research Council at that time (a month ago).

Moreover, in a widely available video, Wolfgang Wodarg—who was chair of the Parliamentary Assembly of the Council of Europe health committee—goes far beyond that, by affirming that we are today measuring not the incidence of disease caused by the virus, but the increasing activity of specialists who are placing it at the centre of their research. But it is not my intention to enter into the debate among scientists concerning the epidemic. I am only interested in the extremely serious ethical and political consequences that derive from it.

"We could argue that, once terrorism ceased to exist as a cause for measures of exception, the invention of an epidemic offers the ideal pretext for widening them beyond all known limits." How can you argue that the epidemic is an invention? Can't terrorism and an epidemic lead to unacceptable political consequences and still be real?

'Invention' in the political sphere should not be understood in a purely subjective sense. Historians know that there are, so to speak, *objective* conspiracies that seem to function as such without being directed by an identifiable subject. As Foucault showed before me, governments that deploy the security paradigm do not necessarily produce the state of exception, but they exploit and direct it once it occurs. I am certainly not alone in thinking that, for a totalitarian government such as China's, the epidemic was the ideal tool for confirming the possibility of isolating and controlling an entire region. And the fact that in Europe it is possible to refer to China as a model to follow only goes to show the degree of political irresponsibility to which fear has reduced us. We should also question the rather suspicious fact that the Chinese government declares the epidemic over whenever it is convenient for it to do so.

Why is the state of exception unjustified, in your opinion, if confinement seems to scientists the only way to contain the spread of the virus?

In the Babelic linguistic confusion of our time, each group of people follows one particular logic, disregarding all others. According to virologists, the enemy is the virus; for doctors, the only goal is recovery;

for the government, it is all about maintaining control—and perhaps I'm also doing the same, when I reiterate that we must refuse to pay too high a price. Europe has seen worse epidemics in the past, but nobody ever thought to declare for this reason a state of exception like the one now in Italy or in France, which effectively prevents people from living. When we consider that the disease has affected less than one in a thousand people in Italy, we can only wonder what will happen if the epidemic worsens. Fear is a bad adviser, and I don't believe that transforming the country into a plague-ridden land, where we all look at each other as potential sources of contagion, is really the solution. The false logic is always the same: just as it was asserted in the face of terrorism that freedom should be abolished in order to defend freedom, now we are told that life has to be suspended in order to protect life.

Are we perhaps witnessing the implementation of a permanent state of exception?

The epidemic has made clear that the state of exception, to which our governments have actually accustomed us for quite some time, has become the normal condition. People are so used to living in conditions of perpetual crisis, that they seem not to realise that their lives have been reduced to a purely biological condition that has lost not only its political dimension, but also that of what is simply human. A society that exists in a perennial state of emergency cannot be free. We live in a society that has sacrificed freedom for so-called 'security reasons' and has hence condemned itself to living in a perpetual state of fear and insecurity.

In what sense are we today living through a 'biopolitical' crisis?

Modern politics is, from top to bottom, biopolitics: what is at stake is, ultimately, biological life as such. The new element is that health is becoming a juridical obligation that has to be fulfilled at all costs.

Why isn't the seriousness of the disease the problem, rather than the ethical and political collapse that the disease has created?

Fear is revealing many of the things that we pretended not to see. The first is that our society believes in nothing beyond bare life. It is clear that Italians are ready to sacrifice practically everything—their normal life conditions, their social relationships, their work, even friendships, as well as their religious and political convictions—when faced with the danger of getting sick. But bare life is not something that unites people: it blinds and separates them. Fellow human beings, as in the plague described by Manzoni in his novel, are now seen only as potential anointers from whom we should maintain a distance of at least one metre, and who should be punished if they get too close to us. The dead, meanwhile—and this is truly barbaric—have no right to a funeral, and it is unclear what happens to their bodies. Our neighbour no longer exists, and it is really bewildering that the two religions that seemed to hold the West together—Christianity and capitalism, the religion of Christ and the religion of money—are keeping quiet on this. What are human relationships becoming in a country which succumbs to living like this?

And what is a society that values nothing above survival?

It is dispiriting to see a whole society dismiss entirely its ethical and political values when faced with what is, after all, an uncertain risk. I don't think it will be able to return to its normal state when all this is over.

How will the world look after the epidemic, in your opinion?

It is not only, and not really, the present but the future that concerns me. Just as wars have bequeathed us a series of nefarious technologies, it is very likely that, after the health emergency is over, governments will attempt to continue the experiments they couldn't previously complete: universities will be closed to students, with classes only being conducted online; we will no longer gather to have conversations about politics or culture; and wherever possible digital devices will replace any contact—any *contagion*—between human beings.

SEVEN

Social Distancing
6 April 2020

It is not certain where Death awaits us, so let us await it
everywhere. To think of death beforehand is to think of
our liberty. Whoever learns how to die has learned how
not to be a slave. Knowing how to die frees us from all
subjection and constraint.

—MONTAIGNE, "THROUGH PHILOSOPHY WE LEARN HOW TO DIE" [3]

Since history teaches us that every social phenomenon
has or can have political implications, we should take
careful note of the new concept that has entered the
West's political lexicon: 'social distancing'. Although
the term was probably conceived as a euphemism after
the rawness of the previous term, 'confinement', we
must ask ourselves what a political order founded on
social distancing could ever amount to. This question
is all the more urgent when such an order may be more
than a purely theoretical hypothesis. It is increasingly
being claimed that the current health emergency can be
seen as the laboratory in which the political and social
orders that await humanity are being prepared.

Though there are, as always, fools who will claim that
such a situation can be considered to be wholly positive,
and that new digital technologies have allowed us hap-
pily to communicate from a distance for some time, I do
not believe that a community based on 'social distancing' is humanly and politically liveable. In any case, it

seems to me that, whatever one's perspective on the matter is, this is the theme upon which we should reflect.

A first consideration is the truly unique nature of the phenomenon that 'social distancing' measures have created. Canetti, in his masterpiece *Crowds and Power*, defines the crowd as the thing upon which power is founded through the inversion of the fear of being touched. While people generally dread being touched by strangers, and while all of the distances they institute around themselves are born of this fear, the crowd is the only setting in which this fear is overthrown.

> It is only in a crowd that man can become free of this fear of being touched. [...] As soon as a man has surrendered himself to the crowd, he ceases to fear its touch. [...] The man pressed against him is the same as himself. He feels him as he feels himself. Suddenly it is as though everything were happening in one and the same body. [...] This reversal of the fear of being touched belongs to the nature of crowds. The feeling of relief is most striking where the density of the crowd is greatest.[4]

I do not know what Canetti would have thought of the new phenomenology of the crowd that we are witnessing. What social distancing measures and panic have created is surely a mass, but a mass that is, so to speak, inverted and composed of individuals who are keeping themselves at any cost at a distance—a non-dense, rarefied mass. It is still a mass, however, if, as Canetti specifies shortly afterwards, it is defined by uniformity and passivity—in the sense that "it is impossible for it to move really freely. [...] [I]t waits. It waits for a head to be shown it."[5]

A few pages later Canetti describes the crowd that is formed through a prohibition, where

a large number of people together refuse to continue to do what, till then, they had done singly. They obey a prohibition, and this prohibition is sudden and self-imposed. [...] [I]n any case, it strikes with enormous power. It is as absolute as a command, but what is decisive about it is its negative character.[6]

We should keep in mind that a community founded on social distancing would have nothing to do, as one might naively believe, with an individualism pushed to excess. It would be, if anything, similar to the community we see around us: a rarefied mass founded on a prohibition but, for that very reason, especially passive and compact.

EIGHT

A Question

13 April 2020

> The plague was the beginning of increased lawlessness in the city. [...] No one was prepared to persevere in what had once been thought the path of honour, as they could well be dead before that destination was reached.
>
> —THUCYDIDES, *THE PELOPONNESIAN WAR*, 2.53[7]

I would like to share with anyone interested a question on which I have been reflecting incessantly for over a month. How did it happen that an entire country, without even realising what was happening, collapsed both ethically and politically in the face of an illness? The words with which I formulate this question have been carefully chosen. The measure of one's abdication of ethical and political principles is very simple: it is a matter of asking oneself what is the limit beyond which one is unwilling to renounce those principles. Readers who think it worth their trouble to consider the following points will, I believe, find it impossible to deny that—without our having even noticed, or perhaps having pretended not to notice—the threshold between humanity and barbarism has been crossed.

i. The first and perhaps most serious point pertains to the bodies of the dead. How did we accept, purely in the name of an indeterminable risk, that our dear ones—and human beings in general—should not only die alone, but that their bodies should be burned without a funeral—something that, from Antigone to the present day, has never happened?

ii. We have also agreed, without making too much of a fuss and, again, purely in the name of an indeterminate risk, to limit our freedom of movement in a manner previously unknown in the country's history—including during the two world wars, when the curfew period was limited to certain hours. Because our neighbour has become a *potential* source of contagion, we have effectively agreed to suspend our friendships and relationships.

iii. This may have happened (and here we are approaching the root of the phenomenon) because we have divided the unity of our vital experience—which is always and inseparably corporeal and spiritual—into a purely biological entity, on the one hand, and a social and cultural life, on the other. Ivan Illich has highlighted—and David Cayley has recently reminded us of—the responsibility of modern medicine for this schism, which, although we take it for granted, is the greatest of all abstractions. Modern science has achieved this abstraction by way of reanimation devices that can keep a body in a state of pure vegetative life. But if this condition is extended beyond the spatial and temporal boundaries that pertain to it—as is presently being attempted—so that it becomes a sort of social behaviour principle, we may fall into inescapable contradictions.

Doubtless someone will rush to respond that what I am describing is a temporally limited condition, after which things will go back to how they were before. It is remarkable that anyone could say this in good faith, given that the very authorities that proclaimed the emergency keep endlessly reminding us that we will have to go on observing the same directives when this is all over, and that 'social distancing' (as it has been euphemistically termed) will be society's new organising principle. In any case, what we have consented to endure—in good or in bad faith—can never be erased.

At this point, and since I have remarked upon everybody else's, I should mention the most serious responsibility of those who ought to have protected human dignity. First of all, the Church. Now a handmaiden of science—the latter having become the true religion of our time—the Church has radically disavowed its most essential principles. Led by a Pope named Francis, it is forgetting that St Francis embraced the lepers. It is forgetting that one of the works of mercy is visiting the sick. It is forgetting the martyrs' teaching that we must be willing to sacrifice life rather than faith, and that renouncing one's neighbour means renouncing faith.

Another group that has failed in its duties is the jurists. We have been accustomed for quite some time to the ill-advised use of emergency decrees through which executive power effectively replaces legislative power—abolishing the separation-of-powers principle that democracy is defined by. In this case, however, all limits have been overstepped: it seems that the words pronounced by the Prime Minister and by the head of the Civil Protection Department have the immediate validity of law (as was once said of the words of the

Führer). It is, furthermore, unclear how the limitations on freedom can be maintained once the temporary validity of the emergency decrees expires. With what juridical apparatuses? With a permanent state of exception? It is the jurists' duty to ensure that the rules of the constitution are respected, but the jurists are silent. *Quare siletis juristae in munere vestro?*[8]

No doubt someone will retort that the sacrifice, serious as it is, has been made in the name of moral principles. I would remind them that Eichmann never failed to reiterate—apparently in good faith—that he did what he did according to his conscience, in order to obey what he believed were the precepts of Kantian morals. A norm which affirms that we must renounce the good to save the good is as false and contradictory as that which, in order to protect freedom, imposes the renunciation of freedom.

NINE

Bare Life
Interview with Ivar Ekman for
Swedish Public Radio, 19 April 2020

Can we consider the current restrictions on social life to be the definitive state of exception? Should we expect that they will remain in place even after the acute phase of this crisis?

The history of the twentieth century—and, in particular, the rise to power of Nazism in Germany—shows clearly that the state of exception is the mechanism by which democracies can transform themselves into totalitarian states. In my country, but not just here, a state of emergency has been the standard governmental procedure for years. Thanks to various emergency decrees, the executive power has superseded the legislative, effectively abolishing the separation-of-powers principle that defines a democracy. Never before, not even under Fascism and during the two world wars, has the limitation of freedom been taken to such extremes: people have been confined to their houses and, deprived of all social relationships, reduced to a condition of biological survival. This barbarity does not even spare the dead: those who die are being deprived of their right to a funeral, their bodies instead burned. Doubtless someone will rush to respond that what I'm describing is only a temporary situation, after which things will go back to how they were before. It is astonishing that anyone could say this in good faith, given that the very authorities which proclaimed the emergency endlessly remind us that, when the emergency is over, we will have to keep observing the same directives, and that 'social distancing' (as it has euphemistically been termed) will be society's new organising principle.

Can you please explain the idea of 'bare life', and how it relates to what is happening today?

You ask about bare life. The truth is that what I'm describing may have happened because we have divided the unity of our vital experience—which is always and inseparably corporeal and spiritual—into a purely biological entity (bare life) on the one hand, and a social and cultural life on the other. Ivan Illich has highlighted modern medicine's responsibility for this schism which, although we take it for granted, is the greatest of all abstractions. Modern science has achieved this abstraction by way of reanimation devices that can keep a body in a state of pure vegetative life. But if this condition is extended beyond the spatial and temporal boundaries that pertain to it—as is presently being attempted—so that it becomes a sort of social behaviour principle, we may fall into inescapable contradictions. Is it really necessary to remind ourselves that the only

39

other place where human beings were kept in a state of pure vegetative life was the Nazi camp?

You belong to a section of the population for which the virus mortality rate seems to be between ten and twenty per cent, and not in the single digits. Are you scared when you encounter other people? Should this fear guide people's behaviours, beyond the rules imposed by authorities?

The risk of contagion, in the name of which freedoms are limited, has never been specifically stated: the numbers communicated are intentionally vague, without any analysis in relation to the annual death rate or the definite causes of death—as would be essential if what was truly at stake was scientific. I will answer you anyways with what Montaigne said: "It is not certain where Death awaits us, so let us await it everywhere. To think of death beforehand is to think of our liberty. Whoever learns how to die has learned how not to be a slave. Knowing how to die frees us from all subjection and constraint."[9]

The political reaction to the virus—the different states of exception—has not been monolithic. There are different models for restricting the lives and movements of people in various parts of the world, and many of these differences can be found even within a single country. In Sweden, most of the limitations are voluntary; our Prime Minister said that people should be guided by their common sense (more precisely, the word he used is 'folkvett', which loosely translates as 'sense of the people'). People do impose limitations on and by

themselves, but many here—and even more in the sur-
rounding states, where the rules are more stringent—re-
acted firmly, calling Swedish leaders irresponsible, as if
the only way to restrain people was through decrees and
through the mobilisation of the police. This is only an
example, but do you think that there could be a reason-
able way to face this threat, beyond the black and white
of a 'death or dictatorship' imperative?

We can only venture hypotheses concerning the forms
that government will assume in the years to come, but
what can be inferred from the current experiments is
not reassuring. Italy, as we witnessed during the years
of terrorism, is a sort of political laboratory where new
technologies of governance are tested. It does not surprise me that Italy is at the moment spearheading the
development of a technology of governance that, in the
name of public health, renders acceptable a set of life
conditions which eliminate all possible political activity, pure and simple. This country is always on the verge
of falling back into Fascism, and there are many signs
today that this is something more than a risk. Suffice
to say that the government has appointed a committee
that has the power to decide which news is true and
which should be considered fake. As far as I myself am
concerned, most major Italian newspapers refuse to
publish my opinions.

TEN

New Reflections[10]
Neue Zürcher Zeitung, 27 April 2020

The hypothesis that we are experiencing the end of a world—the world of bourgeois democracy that is built on rights, parliaments, and the division of powers—is now spreading widely. That world is being replaced by a new despotism that, with the pervasiveness of its controls and with its suspension of all political activity, will be worse than the totalitarianisms we have known thus far. Political commentators call it the 'Security State'—in other words, a state where 'for security reasons' (in this instance for the sake of 'public health', a term that recalls the Reign of Terror's infamous 'Committee of Public Safety') there's no limit to the repression of individual freedoms. In Italy, moreover, we have for some time been getting accustomed to legislation being passed via emergency decrees issued by the executive power, superseding in this manner legislative power and effectively abolishing the separation of powers which is a defining characteristic of democracy. Control exercised through security cameras and, as is now being proposed, through cellphones exceeds by far any form of control exercised under totalitarian regimes such as Fascism or Nazism.

We must also question the ways in which the epidemic's death toll and rates of infection are being communicated. At least as far as Italy is concerned, anyone who knows anything about epistemology cannot but be astonished by the fact that, during these last few months, the media have been broadcasting numbers without exercising any scientific rigour—as they might have done, for example, by comparing them with the annual mortality rate for the same period of time, or even being specific about the causes of death. I am, of course, not an epidemiologist, not even a doctor. I am merely quoting word-for-word official sources that are, surely, reliable. Twenty-three thousand deaths from Covid-19 seems, and certainly is, a startling number. But when compared with annual statistical data, things look rather different. The President of ISTAT (the Italian National Statistics Institute), Dr Gian Carlo Blangiardo, relayed last year's mortality numbers some weeks ago: 647,000 deceased (which is 1,772 deaths daily). If we look at the causes of death in more detail, we observe that the last available data for 2017 registers 230,000 deaths from cardiovascular diseases, 180,000 from cancer, and at least 53,000 from respiratory diseases. One element is particularly important, though, and it affects us directly. I quote here the report:

In March 2019, the deaths caused by respiratory diseases were 15,189; 16,220 in the previous year. It is observed that these numbers are higher than the corresponding number of deaths from Covid (12,352) announced in March 2020.

If this is true—and we have no reason to doubt that it is—then we need to ask ourselves, without underplaying the importance of the epidemic, if it can justify measures that limit our freedoms to an extent never before enforced in the history of this country, not even during two world wars. Legitimate doubts arise concerning Italy: there was, in spreading panic and isolating people in their homes, a decision to burden the citizenry with the grave responsibility governments bear for having dismantled our national healthcare system, and, later, for having made a series of equally serious mistakes when confronting the epidemic in Lombardy. As for the rest of the world, I believe that every state embraces different modalities as it employs the pandemic data for its own ends, manipulating it to suit its specific needs. The real texture of the epidemic can only be ascertained by comparing, in each instance, the communicated data with statistics (categorised by disease) concerning the annual mortality rate.

Another element that we ought to interrogate is the function performed by doctors and virologists in the governance of this epidemic. The Greek term *epidemic* (from *demos*: the people as a political entity) has an immediate political significance. It is dangerous, especially in this light, to entrust doctors and scientists with decisions that are ultimately ethical and political. Rightly or not, scientists pursue in good faith the interests of science and, as history can teach us, they are willing to sacrifice any moral concern in this pursuit. No one will need reminding that, under Nazism, many esteemed scientists executed eugenic policies, never hesitating to take advantage of the camps for the performance of lethal experiments that they considered useful for

44

the progress of science, or for offering care to German soldiers. The spectacle is particularly bewildering in the current case because, in reality, there is no consensus among scientists—even if the media are keeping quiet about this. One of the most illustrious of them has dissenting views on the epidemic's significance, and on the efficacy of the isolation measures: Didier Raoult—perhaps the most important French microbiologist—gave an interview in which he described these measures as a medieval superstition. I have written elsewhere that science has become the religion of our time. The analogy with religion must be read to the letter. Theologians declared that they could not clearly define God, but in his name they dictated rules of behaviour and burned heretics without hesitation; virologists admit that they do not know exactly what a virus is, but in its name they insist on deciding how human beings should live.

If we leave the realm of current events and try to consider things from the perspective of the human species's destiny on earth, the reflections of Louis Bolk, a great Dutch scientist, come to mind. According to Bolk, the human species is characterised by a progressive inhibition of its natural, vital processes of adaptation to its environment. These processes are superseded by a hypertrophic growth of technological apparatuses designed to adapt the environment to mankind. When this process exceeds a certain limit, it becomes counterproductive and transforms itself into the self-destruction of the species. Phenomena such as the one we are currently experiencing indicate that that point has already been reached, and that medicine—which should have cured our sickness—runs the risk of furnishing us with an even greater disease.

ELEVEN

On Truth and Falsity
28 April 2020

Quite predictably, the ministerial decree of Phase 2 more or less confirms the curtailment of constitutional freedoms which ought only to be limited by law. No less important, however, is the limitation placed on a human right that is not enshrined in any constitution: the right to truth, the need for a true word.

What we are now living through is more than just a staggering imposition on everybody's freedoms; it is also a massive campaign to falsify the truth. People consent to limitations on their personal freedoms when they accept the uncorroborated data and opinions conveyed by the media. Advertising has long gotten us used to a discourse that works better when it does not pretend to be true. And for some time, even political consent has been given without the presence of actual conviction—the assumption being that truth is not at stake in electoral speeches. What is currently happening before our eyes is something new, however, if only because we are passively accepting a discourse on whose veracity depends our everyday existence and our entire way of life. It is vital, then, that we examine closely what has been proposed, using just a simple process of verification.

I am not alone in having noticed that the data on the epidemic is offered vaguely and without scientific scrutiny. From an epistemological point of view, it is obvious, for example, that providing the number of deaths without contrasting it with the annual mortality rate for comparable periods and without specifying the real causes of death is meaningless. And yet this is precisely what is happening every day, seemingly without anyone noticing. This gets even more surprising, given that the information that would enable such an investigation is available to anybody who wishes to access it. I have already quoted in this blog the report by the President of ISTAT, Dr Gian Carlo Blangiardo, which confirms that the number of deaths caused by Covid-19 is lower than the number of deaths caused by respiratory diseases in the previous two years. And yet, unequivocal as it is, this account might as well not exist, while, in the meantime, the infected patient who dies from a heart attack or from any other cause is counted as a Covid-related death. Why is there still faith in falsity, even when the falsity is documented? We should say that the lie is held as true precisely because, like advertising, it does not care to hide its falsity. Like the First World War, the war against the virus can only be linked to false and deceitful motives.

Humanity is entering a phase of its history where truth is being reduced to a moment within the march of falsity. That false discourse which must be held as truth *is* true, even when its non-truth is revealed. In this way, it is language itself, as a space for the manifestation of truth, that is being confiscated from us. Now we can only silently observe the unfolding—a *true* development, because it is real—of the lie. And, in order to stop this, we must have the courage to seek, uncompromisingly, the most precious of goods: a true word.

TWELVE

Medicine as Religion
2 May 2020

It has been evident for quite a while that science has become our time's religion, the thing which people believe that they believe in. Three systems of beliefs have coexisted, and in some ways still coexist today, in the modern West: Christianity, capitalism, and science. In the history of modernity these three 'religions' often and unavoidably intersected, each time clashing with one another and then reconciling until they gradually reached a sort of peaceful, articulated *cohabitation* (if not a true *collaboration*, in the name of a common interest).

What is new is that, without us noticing, a subterranean and implacable conflict between science and the other two religions has ignited. Science's triumphs appear today before our very eyes, and they determine in an unprecedented way every aspect of our existence. This conflict does not pertain, as it did in the past, to general theories and principles but, so to speak, to cultic praxis. No less than any other religion, science organises and arranges its own structure through different forms and ranks. To its elaboration of a subtle and rigorous dogmatics corresponds, in praxis, a vast and intricate cultic sphere that coincides with what we call 'technology'.

It is not surprising that the protagonist of this new religious war is the very branch of science whose dogmatics is less rigorous and whose pragmatic aspect is stronger: that is, medicine, whose object is the living human body. Let us try to define the essential features of this victorious faith—one which we will increasingly have to deal with.

i. The first feature is the fact that medicine, like capitalism, has no need for a special dogmatics because it is limited to borrowing its fundamental ideas from biology. Unlike biology, however, medicine articulates these ideas in a Gnostic/Manichean sense; that is to say, through an exacerbated dualistic opposition. There is a malign god or principle—namely, the disease, whose specific agents are, say, bacteria and viruses—and a beneficent god or principle—which is not health, but recovery, whose cultic agents are doctors and therapy. As in every Gnostic faith, these two principles are clearly separated but can, in praxis, contaminate one another: the beneficent principle and the doctor who represents it can err and unknowingly collaborate with their enemy, without thereby invalidating either the reality of the dualism or the cultic necessity through which the beneficent principle fights its battle. It is indeed significant that the theologians who have to entrench this strategy represent a science—virology—that does not possess its own place but stands at the border between biology and medicine.

ii. If until now this cultic practice was, like every other liturgy, episodic and limited in time, the unexpected phenomenon which we are at present witnessing is that it has become permanent and ubiquitous. The cultic practice no longer concerns taking medications, being visited by a doctor, or undergoing surgery. Rather, the entire life of human beings must become, at every instant, the site of an uninterrupted cultic celebration. The enemy (the virus) is omnipresent and must be fought constantly and ceaselessly. The Christian religion knew such totalitarian tendencies as well, but they pertained only to *some* individuals—monks, in particular—who chose to entrust their whole existence to the principle of "pray[ing] without ceasing"[11]. Medicine-as-religion embraces this Pauline precept and, at the same time, reverses it: whereas monks gathered in monasteries in order to pray together, the cult must now be practised no less assiduously but with its devotees also remaining separate and at a distance from one another.

iii. The cultic practice is no longer free or voluntary, nor is it exposed to penalties of a spiritual type: it has become mandatory and legally enforceable. This collusion between religion and profane power is certainly not a novel phenomenon; what is new, however, is the fact that this collusion pertains not to the profession of dogmas—as was the case with heresies— but only to the celebration of the cult. Profane power must be vigilant so that the liturgy of the medical religion—which by now coincides with all of life—is duly observed. It is immediately evident that what is here described is a cultic practice, not a scientific or rational necessity. The most frequent cause of death in our country is, by far, cardiovascular diseases, and it is known that these diseases could be diminished if healthier lifestyles and particular diets were adopted. But to no doctor has it ever occurred that this lifestyle and diet—which are, all the same, *suggested* to patients—could become the object of a legal rule, one that would decree *ex lege* what we should eat and how we should live, transforming our entire existence into a health obligation. And yet this *has* been put in place and, at least for now, people have accepted—as if it were common sense—the renunciation of their freedom of movement, of work, friendships, love, and social relationships, and of their own religious and political beliefs.

We can see here how the two other Western religions—the religion of Christ and the religion of money—have surrendered their primacy to medicine and science, apparently without a fight. The Church has disavowed its principles, pure and simple, forgetting that the saint from whom the current pontiff takes his name used to embrace lepers, that one of the works of mercy is visiting the sick, and that the sacraments can only be administered in person. Capitalism, for its part, has with only a few exceptions accepted losses to productivity that it would have never previously considered, probably hoping that later on it can find an accord with the new religion (which, on this point, seems inclined to yield).

iv. The medical religion has unreservedly adopted from Christianity the eschatological appeal dropped by the latter. Capitalism, by secularising the theological paradigm of salvation, had already eliminated the idea of the end times, replacing it with a permanent state of crisis without redemption or end. 'Krisis' was originally a medical concept which designated, in the Hippocratic corpus of texts, the moment when the doctor decided whether the patient would be able to survive the disease. Theologians reprised the term to indicate the final judgement that occurs during the last day. If we look at the state of exception which we are now experiencing, we could say that the medical religion combines the perpetual crisis of capitalism with the Christian idea of the end times, of an *eschaton* where the extreme decision is constantly ongoing and where the end is simultaneously rushed and deferred in an incessant effort to govern it, without its ever being resolved once and for all. It is the religion of a world that feels itself to be at its end, and yet it cannot—like the Hippocratic doctor—decide whether it will survive or die.

v. Like capitalism, and unlike Christianity, the medical religion offers no prospect of salvation or redemption. On the contrary, the recovery to which it aspires can only be temporary, given that the malignant god—the virus—cannot be annihilated once and for all: it rather mutates constantly, and it always assumes new shapes that are, presumably, ever more hazardous. The epidemic, as the etymology of the term suggests, is first and foremost a political concept that is about to become the new worldwide political—or non-political—terrain. It is quite possible that the epidemic that we are experiencing is the actualisation of a global civil war that, according to the most attentive political analysts, is replacing traditional world wars. All nations and all peoples are now perpetually at war with themselves, because the invisible and elusive enemy that they are fighting is within them.

As has occurred on multiple occasions in the course of history, philosophers will enter again into a conflict with religion—a religion which is no longer Christianity, but science, or that part of science that has assumed the form of a religion. I do not know if the stakes will be reignited or if there will be a list of prohibited books, but certainly the thought of those who keep seeking the truth and rejecting the dominant lie will, as we are already seeing, be excluded and accused of disseminating fake news (news, not ideas, because news is more important than reality!). As in all moments of real or simulated emergency, we will once again see philosophers being slandered by the ignorant, and scoundrels trying to profit from disasters that they themselves have instigated. All this has already happened and will keep happening—but those who speak the truth will never stop doing so, because nobody can bear witness for the witness.

THIRTEEN

Biosecurity and Politics
11 May 2020

What is striking about the reaction to the apparatus of
exception that has been erected in our country and elsewhere is the inability to examine it outside of the immediate context in which it appears to operate. Rarely
does anyone attempt to interpret these new structures,
as any serious political analysis would demand, as
signs and symptoms of a larger experiment in which
a new paradigm for governing people and things is
manifesting itself. In a book published seven years ago
(*Tempêtes microbiennes*, Gallimard, 2013), one that
is now worth rereading carefully, Patrick Zylberman
described the process through which health security,
which until then had been at the margins of political
calculations, was becoming an essential component
of state and international political strategies. What is
at issue is nothing less than the creation of a sort of
'health terror' as a tool for governing the worst-case
scenario[12]. It was according to this logic-of-the-worst
that, as early as 2005, the World Health Organisation

predicted between two and 150 million deaths from the upcoming bird flu, suggesting a political strategy that states were not at that point prepared to embrace. Zylberman shows that the proposed apparatus pivoted on three points: (i) the crafting, on the basis of a potential risk, of a fictitious scenario wherein data would be presented in such a way as to encourage behaviours that would make it possible to govern an extreme situation; (ii) the adoption of the logic-of-the-worst as a regime of political rationality; and (iii) the total organisation of the body of citizens so as fully to reinforce adhesion to governmental institutions, producing a sort of superlative civicism wherein the imposed obligations are presented as proofs of altruism, and where the citizen no longer has a right to health ('health safety') but is instead forced by law to be healthy ('biosecurity').[13]

What Zylberman described in 2013 is exactly what is happening today. It is evident that, beyond the emergency situation associated with a specific virus that will in the future be replaced by another one, what is at stake is the design of a governance paradigm the effectiveness of which exceeds by far that of all other forms of governance that Western political history has ever known. If, amidst the progressive decay of ideologies and political beliefs, security measures had already conditioned citizens to accept limitations on their freedom that they were previously unwilling to accept, biosecurity has proven capable of presenting the absolute cessation of all political activity and social relationships as the highest form of civic participation. We have thus been able to witness the paradox of leftist organisations, traditionally accustomed to

asserting rights and denouncing constitutional viola-
tions, unreservedly accepting limitations on freedom
that were determined—and this is something that even
Fascism did not dare to impose—through legally in-
valid ministerial decrees.

It is evident that—as the same government authorities unceasingly remind us—'social distancing' is the
political model of the future, and that (as has been announced by representatives of a so-called 'task force'
whose members are in a clear conflict of interest in
terms of the function they are supposed to be perform-
ing) this distancing will be taken advantage of in order
to replace human relationships in all their physical
dimension—which has fallen under the suspicion of
contagion (political contagion, it is understood)—with
devices. University classes, as the Ministry of Education, University, and Research has already recommend-
ed, will be held entirely online starting next year; it will
be impossible for us to recognise one another by gazing
at each other's faces—which will have to be covered by
surgical masks—but only through devices that will recognise compulsorily collected biological data; and any
'gathering' held for political reasons—or just for human
fellowship—will remain forbidden.

At issue here is the entire idea of human societal des-
tinies, an idea derived from a perspective that seems for
many reasons to have adopted from our declining religions the apocalyptic idea of an end of the world. Politics has already been superseded by the economy, but
now even the latter, in order for it to govern, will have to
be integrated into the new paradigm of biosecurity—a
paradigm in the name of which all other needs must
be sacrificed. It is legitimate to ask if such a society

can still define itself as human, or if the loss of sensible relationships, of the face, of friendship, of love, can truly be compensated for by an abstract and presumably absolutely fictitious health security.

FOURTEEN

Polemos Epidemios
Interview with Dimitra Pouliopoulou for
Babylonia, 20 May 2020

Epidemics have occurred throughout human history, causing upheavals in societies and in people. The recent coronavirus epidemic will, it seems, be remembered not for its lethality when compared with other epidemics, but for the unprecedented global mobilisation enacted to face it. Much has been written about what is going to happen afterwards. Do you think that this epidemic will represent a rift in the social reality, and that we will talk about 'before' and 'after' the coronavirus era?

I should start by saying that I will mostly be talking about the country I know best, which is Italy. But we should not forget that, since the end of the 1960s, Italy has been the laboratory where new governing technologies have been developed. It is possible that Italy is playing that same role even today with regard to the health emergency.

An epidemic, as is suggested by its etymological roots in the Greek term *demos* (which designates the people as a political body), is first and foremost a political concept. In Homer, *polemos epidemios* is the civil war. What we see today is that the epidemic is becoming the new terrain of politics, the battleground of a global civil war—because a civil war is a war against an internal enemy, one which lives inside of ourselves. We are experiencing the end of an era in the political history of the West, the era of bourgeois democracy founded on constitutions, on rights, on parliaments, and on the division of powers. This model was already facing a crisis: constitutional principles were increasingly being ignored, and the executive power had almost entirely replaced the legislative by operating—as it now does exclusively—through legislative decrees. With the so-called pandemic, things went further: what American political analysts called the 'Security State'—which was established in response to terrorism—has now given way to a health-based paradigm of governance that we term 'biosecurity'. It is important to understand that biosecurity, both in its efficacy and in its pervasiveness, outdoes every form of governance that we have hitherto known. As we have been able to see in Italy—but not only here—as soon as a threat to health is declared, people unresistingly consent to limitations on their freedom that they would never have accepted in the past. We are facing a paradox: the end of all social relations and political activity is presented as the exemplary form of civic participation.

I believe that just a single example clearly shows how deeply the biosecurity regime has transformed all of our democratic political paradigms. In bourgeois democracy, every citizen had a 'right to health'. This right has now been transformed, without anyone noticing, into a legal obligation to be healthy—an obligation that must be fulfilled at all costs. We have seen how high this cost is in the unprecedented measures to which citizens have had to subject themselves.

Thanks to earlier crises, states were already prepared at an institutional level. Policies that had previously been experimented with are now applied on a planetary scale. The term 'war' has been widely used in the context of the current pandemic, while you speak about 'a civil war' because the enemy is within, not outside, ourselves. Which elements of the quarantine do you believe are here to stay? Do you consider the epidemic to be a potential terrain for new politically authoritarian dogmas?

The biosecurity paradigm is not temporary. Economic activity will resume—it already is resuming—and limitations on movement will end, at least for the most part. What will remain is 'social distancing'. We need to think about this singular formulation, which appeared at the same time across the entire world as if it had been prepared in advance. The formula is not 'physical' or 'personal distancing', as it would have been if it was just a medical term, but *'social* distancing'. It could not be communicated more clearly that this is a new paradigm of societal organisation—that is, of an essentially political structure. But what is a society founded on distance? Can we still call such a society 'political'? What sorts of relationships can be established between people who have to keep a one-metre distance, with their faces covered by masks? Distancing was undoubtedly possible to achieve without effort because it was, in some ways, already present. Digital devices have for quite some time gotten us used to distant, virtual relations. The epidemic and technology are here inseparably intertwined. And it is surely no surprise that the head of the so-called task force nominated by the Italian government to face the consequences of the epidemic is the manager of one of the biggest digital communication networks, and that he immediately announced that the implementation of 5G would contribute to the avoidance of any possibility of contagion—in other words, of contact—between human beings. People will no longer recognise one another by looking at each other's faces, which will be covered by sanitary masks, but through digital devices that will identify biometrical data collected in advance. Any 'gathering'—an interesting term for an encounter between human beings—will still be forbidden, whether this 'gathering' is formed for political reasons or simply for the sake of companionship.

In your book, Homo Sacer: Sovereign Power and Bare Life, *you affirm that in every modern state there is a line that delimits the point at which the power over life transforms into power of death, and biopolitics becomes thanatopolitics. On this basis, the sovereign collaborates closely with the lawyer, the doctor, the scientist, the priest. Medicine can today grant to power the possibility—or the illusion—of sovereignty, which affects both the political and the ethical planes. The subordination of life to statistics inevitably leads to the logic of a life that is not worth living, and the political body becomes a biological one. Indeed, in a recent article you highlighted the fact that in the contemporary Western world*

*three 'religions' (Christianity, capitalism, and science)
have coexisted amicably, but that today the conflict between science and the other two religions has reignited,
ending with the victory of science. What is your assess-
ment of the position of scientists, and of medicine in
particular, in the current crisis? And how do you relate
this to the management of power?*

We mustn't underestimate the crucial role that science
and medicine have played in the articulation of the
biosecurity paradigm. As I suggested in the article you
quoted, it was possible for them to exercise this function not as rigorous sciences, but because they act as
a sort of religion whose God is bare life. Ivan Illich,
perhaps the most acute critic of modernity, has shown
how the growing medicalisation of bodies deeply transformed the experience individuals have of their bodies
and their lives. We cannot understand why some human beings have accepted the exceptional restrictions
to which they have been subjected, unless we take this
transformation into account. What has happened is that
individuals have broken the unity of their vital experience—which is always inseparably (and simultaneously)
corporeal *and* spiritual—into a purely biological entity
on the one hand, and a social, cultural, and political existence on the other. All the evidence suggests that this
fracture is an abstraction, but a powerful one. What the
virus has shown clearly is that people believe in this abstraction, and they have sacrificed to it their normal life
conditions, their social relations, their political and religious beliefs, even their friendships and relationships.
    I said that the division of life is an abstraction but, as
you know, modern medicine actualised this abstraction

around the middle of the twentieth century through reanimation devices which made it possible for a human body to be preserved for a long time in a vegetative state. The reanimation room, with its mechanisms of artificial respiration and blood circulation, and its technologies that maintain homeothermy—through which a human body is suspended indefinitely between life and death—is a dark zone that cannot escape its strictly medical boundaries. What happened with the pandemic, however, is that this body, artificially suspended between life and death, has become the new political paradigm by which citizens must regulate their behaviours. The conservation at all costs of bare life, which is abstractly separated from social life, is the most shocking element of the new cult established by medicine-as-religion.

Your concept of the state of exception and of the way in which power is structured has been criticised for its pessimism. In modern capitalistic democracies we are all, according to your theory, potential homines sacri, *while the state of exception has created a context in which sovereignty is becoming an insurmountable condition that societies can barely combat. We would like to hear you comment on this. Additionally, what do you think are the margins of resistance in the current situation, and what is the new that could possibly be born?*

Pessimism and optimism are psychological states that have nothing to do with political analyses: those who use these terms only demonstrate their inability to think. Simone Weil, who thought in an exemplary manner about the transformation of political categories in modernity, wrote during the 1930s a series of articles warning against those who fired themselves up with empty expectations and meaningless words in the face of Fascism's rise in Europe. I believe that today we must seriously ask ourselves whether some of the words that we keep on using—such as democracy, legislative power, elections, constitution—actually lost their original meaning a long time ago.

Only if we succeed in gazing lucidly at the new forms of despotism that have replaced those words will we be able to define new forms of resistance with which to oppose that despotism.

In the last few years, the refugee question has emerged as a major problem that humanity is being asked to face. The relocation of populations under current conditions is historically comparable, at least in numerical terms, to what happened after the two world wars. Both Greece and Italy, given their geopolitical positions, are experiencing with a particular intensity the issue of the violent expatriation of huge populations from the East to the West. In a text titled "Beyond Human Rights" you indicated that the Declaration of Rights represents the point at which the transition from divine sovereignty to national sovereignty (based on birth, since natio *means 'birth' in Latin) takes place. Life hence gets integrated into the sphere of state sovereignty. The transformation of the subject of monarchy into the citizen involves the transformation of natural bare life (that is, of birth) into a body that incorporates and founds sovereignty. The principle of birth and the principle of sovereignty, which under the* ancien régime *were divided, are now irrevocably united for the purpose of establishing the*

65

foundation of the new nation state. We are, therefore, faced with the identification of birth with nation, while access to rights can be attributed to man only when he is registered as a citizen in the sphere of statal sovereignty. Refugees represent the breaking point between birth and nationality: they break the identification between man and citizen, and they therefore cause a crisis in the dominant narrative—that is, in the state-nation-territory triptych. The European strategy towards refugees is today carried out through war cries—using countries such as Greece, Turkey, and Libya as deposits of souls. In the aforementioned text you underline the urgent need for a redefinition of the concept of citizenship in the European world—one that will enable a smoother integration of these populations. We would like you to comment on this issue.

In the text you are quoting I attempted, following an article by Hannah Arendt entitled "We Refugees", to juxtapose the figures of the refugee and the citizen as a founding political paradigm.[14] My intention was to interrogate the meaning of the 1789 Declaration of Rights—and of its reprisal in the twentieth century— with its ambiguous distinction/identification between man and citizen. And, just as Arendt wrote that refugees were actually the avant-garde of their people, I similarly proposed to replace the citizen with the refugee as the foundation of a new horizon of politics, one whose urgency is already inescapable. The idea of citizenship, which from Athens through to modernity was at the centre of the political life of the city, has in recent decades been progressively emptied of any real political content. Under the influence of the biopolitical dimension, and later with the establishment of the security paradigm, citizenship became an increasingly passive condition, subjected to a growing and ubiquitous control.

Under the new biosecurity paradigm that is being implemented before our very eyes, the idea of citizenship has completely changed, and the citizen has become the passive object of medical treatment, controls, and of all kinds of suspicion. The pandemic has shown beyond doubt that citizens are being reduced to their bare biological existences. In this way, the citizen resembles the figure of the refugee, and the two almost blend together. The refugee by now inhabits the body of the citizen. A new civil war is hence delineated: the new enemy is, like the virus, inside one's own body. And, as usually happens when our antagonist bears too close a resemblance to ourselves, the civil war will become more ferocious, and without any possible respite.

The extreme situation created by the epidemic caused an atmosphere of panic. The response came mainly from nation states and not really from international organisations, which were very confused about possible courses of action. The expansion of globalisation for individuals and for society, but also the incapacity of the sovereign to legitimise the foundations of power, seemed to eliminate the role of nation states in political management, elevating the market as the sole regulatory factor. Today, in the face of the epidemic, the concept of leadership has been reinforced, and state rulers present themselves as society's saviours—this is what we are witnessing in Greece. What do you think the condition of the nation state will be after the pandemic?

My archaeological enquiries into the history of Western politics have shown me that the system which those politics establish is always bipolar. In a rightly famous book, Karl Polanyi demonstrated that, already during the first Industrial Revolution, market ideology, while seemingly contraposed to state power, was in reality working in conjunction with it: only through this secret collaboration could market ideology bring about the great transformation of Western society. State power has always, in every era, coexisted with new forces inside or outside of it: this is true for both the duality between temporal and spiritual power in the Middle Ages, and the antagonism between workers' movements and state organisation in the twentieth century. When we talk today about globalisation, big spaces, and the resulting eclipse of the nation state, it should not be forgotten that this apparent antithesis will result not in the abolition of state powers, but in their transformation. The bipolar system that defines Western politics will keep working in new forms. The pandemic has shown clearly that an undoubtedly global strategy like the one planned by the World Health Organisation and Bill Gates—from whom the WHO, in reality, emanates—cannot be achieved without the crucial intervention of nation states: they are the only ones who can take, as indeed they did, the coercive measures that such a strategy requires. The epidemic—which always recalls a certain *demos*—is thus inscribed in a pandemic, where the *demos* is no longer a political body but, instead, a biopolitical population.

We have recently read some articles in the German press that raise the following question: which form of government has better faced the pandemic crisis?

Democracy or despotism? The Aristotelian question regarding the ideal state—a question that has long been subjected to the triumphant supremacy of liberal democracy—is cautiously returning. Will the criticism of the liberal and globalised status quo be forced to go through authoritarian and centralised channels, or is there a perspective capable of recreating a democratic politics beyond the state and the market?

The fact that a totalitarian state can be taken as a model in the face of an epidemic shows how far political irresponsibility can go. The mistake here is not in raising the question of the possible inadequacy of the democratic system. Heidegger, in a different context, had already asked (not unadvisedly) if democracy was the appropriate political form in the face of the ubiquity of technology. The mistake lies in framing the choice as one between democracy and despotism. We need to conceptualise an alternative political configuration that could escape the eternal oscillation—one that we have been witnessing for decades—between a democracy that degenerates into despotism and a totalitarianism that is shaped in an apparently democratic form. We already know, thanks to Tocqueville, that democracy has a tendency to deteriorate into despotism; for a careful observer it is difficult to decide whether we live today, in Europe, in a democracy that uses increasingly despotic forms of control, or in a totalitarian state disguised as a democracy. It is beyond both that a new, future politics will have to appear.

In your most recent interventions, you've criticised the state administration for its management of the pandemic, more specifically for imposing prohibitive measures and for banning many social activities. But these measures have been embraced with evident caution, if not with hostility, by a significant number of government officials. The characteristic examples are Donald Trump, Jair Bolsonaro, Boris Johnson, dictators such as Alexander Lukashenko, and of course many international market actors. How do you assess this aversion towards prohibitive measures as expressed by some sections of the international elite?

The degree of confusion into which the emergency situation has thrown the minds of those who ought to remain lucid, and the way in which the opposition between the Right and the Left has become devoid of any real political content, is very clear in this case. A truth remains such, whether it is expressed by the Left or enunciated by the Right. If a fascist says that '2+2=4', this is not an objection against mathematics. Along similar lines, a radical leftist movement in Germany called, significantly, Demokratischer Widerstand (democratic resistance) has recently been attacked by the media while rightly protesting against the violation of constitutional freedoms, because it shares those concerns with the extreme Right. One of the organs of the dominant system, *Der Spiegel*, interviewed me to ascertain my view on this situation, given that the aforementioned movement explicitly referenced my name. When I declared that I had nothing to do with that group but that I nevertheless believed that they had the right to express their opinion and that the extreme Right's similar claims were not invalidating, the *Der Spiegel* journalist—in line with the magazine's characteristic bad habits—simply cut my answer, publishing only its first half.

It is crucial in these cases to analyse the reasons that have led the political leaders you mentioned to profess one particular opinion rather than another, and to examine the strategies by which an idea that is correct in itself is deployed—without questioning that idea's truth.

FIFTEEN

Requiem for the Students
24 May 2020

As we predicted, university classes will be held online next year. What was evident to the attentive observer—that the so-called pandemic would be used as pretext for an increasingly pervasive diffusion of digital technologies—has duly happened.

We are not interested here in the resulting transformation of teaching, through which the element of physical presence—always so important to the relationship between students and teachers—is disappearing once and for all, along with collective discussions in seminars—the most lively part of teaching. One aspect of the technological barbarity we are experiencing is the erasure of every sensory experience and the loss of the gaze, which is now lastingly imprisoned in a spectral screen.

A much more crucial aspect of what is happening is, significantly, going unnoticed: the end of student life as a form of existence. Universities were born in Europe from student associations (*universitates*), whence derives their name. Being a student was, first and foremost, a form of life, one to which studying and listening to lectures were certainly fundamental, but to which encountering and constantly exchanging ideas with other *scholarii*, who often came from the most remote locations and who would gather in *nationes* according to their places of origin, was no less important. This form of life evolved in various ways over the course of centuries. Nevertheless, the social dimension of the phenomenon remained constant from the *clerici vagantes* in the Middle Ages to the student movements of the twentieth century. Those who have taught in university classrooms will know how friendships are formed before one's very eyes and how small study groups, organised around shared cultural and political tendencies, end up meeting after the end of class.

All this, which lasted for almost ten centuries, is now ending—forever. Students will no longer live in the cities that host their universities; they will instead listen to classes from the confinement of their own rooms, sometimes separated by hundreds of kilometres from those who would have once been their peers. Small cities and prestigious university towns will witness the disappearance of student communities from their streets, and thus will be deprived of some of their most vital elements.

Of every social phenomenon that dies it can be said that it somehow deserved its end. It is certain that our universities had reached such a level of corruption and specialistic cluelessness that it is almost impossible to mourn their loss. The students' quality of life was correspondingly impoverished. But there are two points that remain central:

i. The instructors who agree—as they have done *en masse*—to subject themselves to the new online dictatorship and to hold all their classes remotely are the exact equivalent of those university professors who, in 1931, pledged allegiance to the Fascist regime. As in that case, probably only fifteen out of a thousand will refuse to submit. Their names, however, will certainly be remembered alongside the names of those who did not swear allegiance to Fascism.

ii. Students who really love studying will have to refuse to enrol in these transformed universities and, as their counterparts did centuries ago, establish themselves in new *universitates*. Only there, against this technological barbarity, can the word of the past be kept alive and something like a new culture be born—if it ever is born.

SIXTEEN

Two Notorious Terms
10 July 2020

Two notorious terms have emerged out of the debates that happened during this health emergency. It was obvious that their only purpose was to discredit those who kept thinking in defiance of the fear that paralysed all thought. These terms are 'denier' and 'conspiracy theorist'. It is not worth saying much about the first term. Those who use it incautiously equate the current epidemic with the Holocaust, demonstrating (consciously or not) the antisemitism that runs rampant in both Left and Right discourse. As some rightly offended Jewish friends of mine have suggested, it might be opportune for the Jewish community to comment on this ignoble terminological abuse.

It is, however, worth pausing over the second term, which demonstrates a genuinely surprising historical ignorance. Those who are familiar with historiography know that the stories that historians retrace and narrate are, by their nature, often the result of the plans and actions of individuals, groups, and factions who pursue their goals using all means available to them. Below are three examples from among thousands. Each of them has marked the end of an era and the beginning of a new historical period.

In 415 BC, Alcibiades deployed his prestige, his riches, and every possible expedient in order to convince the Athenians to embark on an expedition to Sicily. That expedition would later reveal itself to be a complete disaster, and it coincided with the end of Athenian supremacy. For their part, Alcibiades's enemies—taking advantage of the vandalisation of the statues of Hermes that had occurred a few days before the expedition—hired false witnesses and conspired against him in order to condemn him to death for impiety.

On the Eighteenth Brumaire (9 November 1799), Napoleon Bonaparte—despite his oath of fidelity to the Constitution of the Republic—overthrew the Directory in a coup and was proclaimed First Consul with full powers, thereby ending the Revolution. Days before, Napoleon had met with Sieyès, Fouché, and Lucien Bonaparte so that they could fine-tune their strategy against the anticipated opposition of the Council of Five Hundred.

The March on Rome by approximately 25,000 fascists took place on 28 October 1922. In the months leading up to the event, Mussolini (who prepared the march with the future triumvirs De Vecchi, De Bono, and Bianchi) initiated contact with the Prime Minister (Luigi Facta), with D'Annunzio, and with figures from the business world—according to some, Mussolini even met secretly with the King—so as to probe possible allegiances. In a sort of rehearsal, fascists militarily occupied Ancona on 2 August.

In each of these three cases, individuals gathered in groups or parties and acted resolutely to achieve their goals, considering various possible circumstances and adapting their strategies accordingly. Chance undoubtedly played a role, as in every human event, but trying to explain history through chance is meaningless, and no serious historian has ever undertaken such a pointless endeavour. This does not mean that it is always necessary to speak about 'conspiracies'. But anyone who labelled a historian who tried to reconstruct in detail the plots that triggered such events as a 'conspiracy theorist' would most definitely be demonstrating their own ignorance, if not idiocy.

It is even more astonishing, in this light, that such attitudes persist in a country like Italy, where our recent history is nothing if not the result of intrigues, secret societies, ploys, and conspiracies of all kinds, and to such an extent that historians cannot get to the bottom of many of the decisive events of the last fifty years— from the Piazza Fontana bombing to the murder of Aldo Moro. This is, in fact, so true that Francesco Cossiga, a former President of the Republic, declared that he was an active member of Gladio, one of these secret societies.

As for the pandemic, serious research has shown that it did not arrive unexpectedly. As Patrick Zylberman's book *Tempêtes microbiennes* (Gallimard, 2013) crucially documents, the World Health Organisation suggested a scenario similar to the present one as early as 2005 (during the bird flu), and it furthermore proposed it to governments as a way of ensuring citizens' unconditional support! Bill Gates, who is the WHO's main financier, has made his thoughts on the risks of a pandemic known on many occasions: he warned that a pandemic threatened to cause millions of deaths and that it was therefore necessary to guard against it. As a result, and in the context of research funded by the Bill & Melinda Gates Foundation, the Johns Hopkins Center for Health Security organised in 2019 a simulation exercise for the coronavirus pandemic called "Event 201". This exercise gathered experts and epidemiologists to prepare a coordinated response in the event of a new virus appearing.

In this case, as has indeed occurred throughout history, there are people and organisations pursuing licit or illicit objectives and then trying to realise those objectives by any means necessary. For those who wish to understand what is happening it is vital to know and think about these tendencies. For this reason, speaking of a conspiracy adds nothing to the reality of facts. Defining anyone who seeks to know historical events for what they really are as a 'conspiracy theorist', however, is plain defamation.

SEVENTEEN

Law and Life
(Unpublished)

The current situation, where health has become the epi-
centre of all that is at stake in law and in politics, is
an opportunity to think about the relations that ought
to obtain between law and life. Yan Thomas, a distinguished historian of Roman law, has shown how, in
Roman jurisprudence, nature and the natural life of
human beings never enter *as such* into legal discourse
but are, rather, separated from it—functioning only
as a fictional premise for a legal situation. The principle that 'all things are common'—namely, that the air,
the sea, and the shores are excluded from the realm
of private property—is therefore true only as a limitation: the thing that is 'common to all' can immediately
become the *res nullius* on which the proprietorship of
the first person who seizes it is established. Citizenship
is, correspondingly, an imprescriptible and ineluctably
legal status that, unlike the *domicilium* (which depends
on physical residence in a certain place), is obtained
through *origo*—which is not, as one might think, the

natural fact of birth but, rather, a legal construction connected to one's father's birthplace.

Nineteenth-century jurists transformed this legal artifice into *ius sanguinis*, under which, as Yan Thomas writes, a "mystique of blood, leading to today's prominent biological ideology, replaces what was once only a fictional genealogical construction"[15]. From the first decades of the twentieth century, the law tended towards the incorporation of life, by making life its own specific object—either to protect, or to exclude it. Law taking on living does not only have, as one might expect, positive consequences: in fact, it paves the way for the most extreme risks. As Foucault's work has shown, biopolitics tends fatally to morph into *thanatopolitics*. As the law begins to deal explicitly with the biological life of citizens as a good that needs taking care of, this interest immediately takes a dark turn towards the idea of a life that is, as the title of a well-known work published in Germany in 1920 puts it, "unworthy of life [*lebensunwertes Leben*]"[16].

Every time a value is ascertained, a non-value is, necessarily, established: the flipside of protecting health is excluding and eliminating everything that can give rise to disease. We should reflect carefully on the fact that the first case of legislation by means of which a state programmatically assumed for itself the care of its citizens' health was Nazi eugenics. Soon after his rise to power in July 1933, Hitler promulgated a law for the protection of the German people from hereditary diseases. This led to the creation of special hereditary health courts (*Erbgesundheitsgerichte*) that decreed the forced sterilisation of 400,000 people. Less well known is that, long before Nazism, a eugenic politics was planned in the United States—particularly in California—with robust funding from the Carnegie Institute and the Rockefeller Foundation, and that Hitler explicitly referenced this model. If health becomes the object of a state politics transformed into biopolitics, then it ceases to concern itself first and foremost with the agency of each individual and becomes, instead, an obligation which must at any cost, no matter how high, be fulfilled.

Just as Yan Thomas warned that law and life must not be conflated, so too should law and medicine be kept separate. Medicine has the task of addressing ailments according to the principles irrevocably sanctioned by the Hippocratic Oath, principles which it has followed for centuries. If medicine, making a necessarily ambiguous and indeterminate pact with governments, presents itself instead as a legislator, not only does this *not* lead to positive results in the field of health—as we have witnessed in Italy during the pandemic—but it can result in unacceptable limitations on individual freedom. It should be evident to everybody that the medical reasons behind these limitations could offer the ideal pretext for an unprecedented control over social life.

EIGHTEEN

State of Emergency
and State of Exception
30 July 2020

In a recently published newspaper article, a jurist whom I used to think highly of tried to justify, with arguments that aspire to be legal, the state of exception that has once again been declared by the government. In an implicit reference to the Schmittian distinction between commissary dictatorship—whose aim is to conserve or restore the constitution—and sovereign dictatorship—which seeks, instead, to establish a new order—said jurist distinguishes between emergency and exception (or, as would be more apt, between the state of emergency and the state of exception).

This argument does not, in fact, have any legal grounding: no constitution can possibly foresee its legitimate subversion. This is why Schmitt in his work *Political Theology*, where we find the famous definition of the sovereign as "he who decides on the exception"[17], rightly and simply speaks of the *Ausnahmezustand*—the state of exception—which, in German discourse and beyond, became the technical term for defining the 'no man's land' between the legal order and the political fact, between law and its suspension.

Following the first Schmittian distinction, the jurist claims that the emergency is conservational, while the exception is innovational. "An emergency is used to return as soon as possible to normality [...]; the exception is instead used to break the rule and to establish a new order." The state of emergency "presupposes the stability of a system; the exception, on the other hand, its decline—which opens the way to a different system."

All the evidence suggests that the distinction is a political and sociological one: it refers to a personal evaluation of the state of the system in question, of its stability or decay, and of the intentions of those who have the power to decree a suspension of the law—a suspension that, from a legal standpoint, is essentially identical in the state of emergency and the state of exception, given that both states resolve into the pure and simple suspension of constitutional guarantees. Whatever its goals may be—goals that nobody can presume to evaluate clearly—there is only one state of exception and, once it is declared, there are no possible procedures that have the power to assess the reality or the gravity of the conditions that determined it. It is not by chance that the jurist at one point feels the need to write: "[i]t is undoubtable to me that we are currently facing a health emergency." This is a subjective judgement, interestingly expressed by someone who can claim no medical authority, and to which it is possible to submit many opposing judgements that are certainly more reliable—all the more so since, as he admits, "conflicting voices are coming from the scientific community". The decisional power is, therefore, ultimately in the hands of whoever can declare the emergency. He continues by stating that, unlike the state of exception, which is defined by indeterminate powers, the state of emergency "includes only the powers directed toward the predetermined goal of returning to normality". And yet he immediately afterwards concedes that such powers "cannot be specified preemptively". One need not possess vast legal expertise to realise that, from the point of view of the suspension of constitutional guarantees—which should, indeed, be the only relevant point of view—there is no difference between the two states.

The jurist's argument is doubly deceptive: not only does it introduce a factitious legal distinction but, in order to justify at all costs the state of exception declared by the government, its author is also forced to resort to factual and debatable arguments that fall outside his expertise. This is even more surprising when he ought to know that, in what he considers to be a mere state of emergency, rights and constitutional guarantees that had never previously been questioned—not even during the two world wars—have now been suspended and violated. The fact that this is not a temporary situation is expressed vehemently by the same rulers who endlessly reiterate that not only has the virus not disappeared, but that it can reappear at any time.

At the end of the article, perhaps with a last grain of intellectual honesty, the jurist mentions the view of those who, "not without good arguments, think that, the virus aside, the entire world lives anyway, and in a more or less stable manner, in a state of exception", and that "the social-economic system of capitalism" is unable to face its own crises within the framework of the rule of law. With this perspective in mind, he concedes that "the pandemic that keeps entire societies hostage is a coincidence and an unexpected opportunity, one to be seized upon in order to control oppressed people". Allow me to invite him to think more carefully about the state of the society in which he lives, and to remind him that jurists are not—despite the fact that for a long time they unfortunately have been—just bureaucrats onto whom falls the onus of justifying the system in which they live.

NINETEEN

The Face and the Mask

8 October 2020

[…] what is called the countenance, which can exist in no animate being besides the human being, indicates character.

—CICERO, *DE LEGIBUS*, 1.27[18]

All living beings are in a state of openness—they show themselves and communicate with one another—but only human beings have a face. Only for a human being is one's own appearance and communication to others a fundamental experience; only human beings make their faces the site of their own truth.

What the face exposes and reveals is not something that can be put into words, not something that can be formulated in a signifying proposition. It is in their faces that humans unwillingly drop their guard; it is in the face—and before any words are spoken—that they express and reveal themselves. And what the face expresses is not only an individual's emotional state but, first and foremost, their openness, their exposure, and their communication to others.

This is why the face is the site of politics. If there are no animal politics, it is only because animals, who are always and already in openness, do not take issue with their exposure—they simply dwell in it without worrying about it. This is why they are not interested in mirrors or in the image as such. Men, on the contrary, want to recognise themselves and to be recognised; they want to grasp their own image, they seek their truth in it. In this way they transform their openness into a world, into the field of incessant political dialectics.

If individuals only had to communicate information, this thing or that thing, there would never be proper politics, but only an exchange of messages. But since they must first communicate their openness—in other words, a pure communicability—the face is the very condition of politics, the site on which everything that individuals say and communicate is founded. The face is, in this sense, the true city of men, the fundamental political element. It is by looking at their faces that individuals recognise themselves and develop a passion for one another; it is how they perceive affinity and diversity, distance and proximity.

A country that decides to renounce its face, to cover with masks the faces of its citizens everywhere is, then, a country that has purged itself of any political dimension. Inhabiting this empty space, which is at every moment subjected to a control which knows no limits, individuals now live in isolation from one another. They have lost the immediate and sensible foundation of their community, and they can only exchange messages directed towards a name that no longer possesses a face. A faceless name.

TWENTY

What Is Fear?

13 July 2020

What *is* fear, into which people today seem to have fallen so deeply that they have forgotten their ethical, political, and religious beliefs? It is surely something familiar and yet, at the same time, if we attempt to define it, it seems to obstinately evade comprehension.

In Par. 30 of *Being and Time*, Heidegger offers an exemplary discussion of fear as a mode of attunement. Fear can only be understood if we begin with the fact that *Dasein* (the term Heidegger uses to refer to the existential structure of man) is always already rooted in attunement—the latter describing Dasein's originary openness to the world. Since attunement is this originary openness to and discovery of the world, consciousness is always already anticipated by it. Consciousness can, therefore, neither dispense with attunement nor expect that it can master it. Attunement should not be confused with a psychological state—it is, ontologically, the openness that has always already shown man in his being-in-the-world-ness. Only through attunement are experiences, affections, and knowledge possible: "reflection can find 'experiences' only because the there is already disclosed in attunement"[19]. A mood may assail us, yet "[i]t comes neither from 'without' nor from 'within', but rises from being-in-the-world itself as a mode of that being"[20]. However, this openness does not mean that what it is being revealed to is recognised as such. On the contrary, openness makes manifest just a naked facticity: "[t]he pure 'that it is' shows itself, the whence and the whither remain obscure".[21] This is why Heidegger can say that attunement opens the *there* precisely in "the *thrownness* [...] of [...] being into its there"[22]. The openness that occurs in attunement is, in other words, a being-given-over to something that cannot be assumed and which it vainly attempts to escape.

This is evident in bad moods, in boredom, and in depression. Like any other attunement, they disclose Dasein "more primordially, but [they] also *close* [...] it off more stubbornly, than any *not*-perceiving"[23]. So, in depression, "Dasein becomes blind to itself, the surrounding world of heedfulness is veiled, the circumspection of taking care is led astray"[24]. Even in this case, however, Dasein is consigned to a disclosure from which it cannot possibly free itself.

It is in the context of this ontology of attunement that we should situate our analysis of fear. Heidegger starts by examining three aspects of that phenomenon: the 'before which' (*Wovor*) of fear, the 'fearing itself' (*Fürchten*), and the 'about which' (*Worum*) of fear. The 'before which', the object of fear, is always something intramundane. What is frightening is always—whatever its nature—something within the world and as such it has a dangerous and threatening nature. It can be more or less known and nonetheless "'unnerving' ['*geheuer*']"[25], and it is placed within a determinate nearness however far away it is.

> As something threatening, what is harmful is not yet near enough to be dealt with, but it is coming near. As it approaches, harmfulness radiates and thus has the character of threatening. [...] As something approaches in nearness [...] what is harmful is threatening, it can get us, and yet perhaps not. [...] [W]hat is harmful, approaching near, bears the revealed possibility of not happening and passing us by. This does not lessen or extinguish fearing, but enhances it.[26]

(This 'certain uncertainty' which characterises fear is also evident in Spinoza's definition: an "intermittent pain [...] arising from the image of a dubious event"[27].)

As for the second characteristic of fear, 'fearing itself', Heidegger specifies that "[i]t is not that we initially ascertain a future evil (*malum futurum*) and then are afraid of it"[28]. Rather, the fearsomeness of the thing approaching us is discovered at the outset.

> As a dormant possibility of attuned being-in-the-world, fearing, 'fearfulness' has already disclosed the world with regard to the fact that something like a fearful thing can draw near to us from this fearfulness. The ability to draw near is itself freed by the essential, existential spatiality of being-in-the-world.[29]

Fearfulness as originary disclosedness of Dasein always precedes any determinable fear.

Lastly, regarding that 'about which' fear is afraid, it is always the same being that feels fear, the Dasein, this determined man that is at question.

> Only a being which is concerned in its being about that being can be afraid. Fearing discloses this being in its jeopardization, in its being left to itself.[30]

Being afraid for our own house, for our property, or for others, does not challenge this diagnosis. It can be said that we are 'fearful' for someone else without our being truly scared, but if we actually feel afraid it *is* for ourselves, because we fear that the other could be "snatched away from us"[31].

In this sense, fear is a fundamental mode of attunement that shows humans in their being as always already exposed and threatened. Naturally, this threat has different degrees: if something threatening, which is in front of us with its "not right now, but at any moment"[32] character, suddenly hits this being, fear becomes alarm (*Erschrecken*); if what is threatening is not already known but is instead profoundly unfamiliar, fear becomes horror (*Grauen*). When something threatening combines both, then fear becomes terror (*Entsetzen*). In any case, all these different forms of attunement show that man, in his own disclosedness, is fundamentally fearful.

The only other attunement that Heidegger analyses in *Being and Time* is anxiety. And it is to anxiety, and not to fear, that the status of 'fundamental' attunement is attributed. But it is specifically in relation to fear that Heidegger is able to define the nature of anxiety, by determining at the outset "[h]ow [...] what anxiety is anxious about [is] phenomenally differentiated from what fear is afraid of [...]"[33]. While fear always has to do with *something*, "[w]hat anxiety is about is not an innerworldly being"[34]. Not only is the perceived threat potentially harmless, but

> [w]hat anxiety is about is completely indefinite. This indefiniteness not only leaves factically undecided which innerworldly being is threatening, it also means that innerworldly beings in general are not 'relevant' [...].[35]

What anxiety is about is not a being, but the world as such. That is to say, anxiety is "the world in its worldliness"[36]:

> only because anxiety always already latently determines being-in-the-world, can being-in-the-world [...] be afraid. Fear is anxiety which has fallen prey to the 'world'. It is inauthentic and concealed from itself as such.[37]

It has been rightly observed that the primacy of anxiety over fear affirmed by Heidegger can easily be reversed: instead of defining fear as a diminished anxiety which has fallen into an object, we can legitimately define anxiety as a fear deprived of its object. If the object is taken away from fear, fear is transformed into anxiety. In this sense, fear would then be the fundamental attunement into which man is already and always at risk of falling. Hence its essential political meaning—going back at least as far as Hobbes—which constitutes fear as that by which power is both established and justified.

Let's try to unpack and develop Heidegger's analysis. It is significant, in the present context, that fear always refers to a 'thing', to an intramundane being (in the present case to a virus, the tiniest of beings). Its intramundane nature means that it has lost any relation with openness to the world, and that it exists factitiously and inexorably without the possibility of transcendence. If the structure of being-in-the-world implies for Heidegger a transcendence and an openness, it is this same transcendence that delivers Dasein to the sphere of thinghood. Being-in-the-world means, in fact, being co-originally restored to the things that that openness to the world reveals. While the animal, without a world, cannot perceive an object as such, man, in opening to a world, can be assigned to a thing as a thing without escape.

This leads to the originary possibility of fear: it is the attunement disclosed when man, losing the nexus between the world and things, finds himself irremissibly consigned to intramundane beings and cannot figure out his relationship with a 'thing', which now becomes threatening. Once his relationship to the world is lost, the 'thing' becomes in itself terrorising. Fear is the dimension into which humanity falls when consigned, as has happened in modernity, to an unavoidable thingness. The fearsome being, the 'thing' that attacks and threatens people in horror movies, is thus nothing more than an incarnation of this inescapable thingness.

This also brings out the feeling of impotence that defines fear. Those who feel fear try in every way and by every means to protect themselves from the thing that threatens them—by wearing a mask, for example, or by staying at home. This does not reassure them, however, but on the contrary renders their impotence against the 'thing' even more palpable and constant. Fear can in this light be defined as the opposite of the will to power. The essential character of fear is a will to impotence, a wanting-to-be-impotent in the face of the fearsome thing. Likewise, those who feel fear seek reassurance from those who are recognised as possessing some authority (doctors, civil protection officials, etc.), but this does not in any way get rid of the feeling of insecurity that accompanies fear—which is an essential element of the will to insecurity, the wanting-to-be-insecure. The truth of this is evident from the fact that the very subjects whose responsibility it is to reassure are those who, instead, perpetuate insecurity. They tirelessly repeat, for the good of the frightened, that the object of their fear can never be defeated or eliminated.

How is one to deal with this fundamental attunement, in which man seems always and constitutively to be in the act of collapsing? Since fear precedes and forestalls knowledge and reflection, it is quite useless to try and convince the frightened with rational arguments and evidence; more than anything, fear denies them access to a reasoning process that would preclude fear itself. As Heidegger writes, fear "bewilders us and makes us 'lose our heads'"[38]. So much so that, in the face of the epidemic, it was evident that the publication of irrefutable data and opinions from trustworthy sources was being systematically ignored and discarded in favour of others that, by the way, did not even feign scientific credibility.

Given the originary character of fear, the only way we can ever untangle it is by accessing an equally originary dimension. Such a dimension does exist: it is an openness to the world in which only things can appear and threaten us. Things become fearsome because we

94

forget their co-belonging to a world that transcends them and, at the same time, makes them present. The only possibility of severing the 'thing' from the fear from which it seems inseparable lies in remembering that openness in which it has always and already been exposed and revealed. Not reasoning, but memory—remembering ourselves and our being-in-the-world—is what grants us again access to a thingness that is free from fear. This 'thing' that terrifies me, invisible to the eye though it is, is as open in its pure existence as are all other intramundane beings—this tree, this stream, this man. Only because I am in the world can things appear to me and, potentially, scare me. They are a part of my being-in-the-world, and it is this fact—rather than a thingness abstractly separate and wrongfully established as sovereign—which dictates the ethical and political rules of my behaviour. Of course, the tree may break and fall on me, the stream can overflow and flood the town, and this man can unexpectedly hit me. If these contingencies materialise, a proportionate level of concern will dictate the appropriate course of action. No need to lose our heads, no need to let anyone exercise power on the basis of fear or, by transforming an emergency into a permanent state, to rewrite the rules that guarantee our freedom and determine what we can and cannot do.

TWENTY-ONE

On the Time to Come
23 November 2020

What is happening today on a global scale is certainly the end of a world. But it is not—as it is for those who are trying to govern in accordance with their own interests—an end in the sense of being a transition to a world that is better suited to the new needs of the human consortium. The era of bourgeois democracy, with its rights, its constitutions, and its parliaments, is fading. But beyond this surface-level legal transformation, which is certainly not irrelevant, what is ending is, primarily, the world that began with the Industrial Revolution and built up to the two—or three—world wars and to the totalitarianisms—tyrannical or democratic—that accompanied them.

If the powers that govern the world believed that they had to resort to measures and apparatuses as extreme as biosecurity and the health terror—which they have established everywhere and without any scruples (but which are now getting out of hand)—this is because, as all the evidence suggests, they feared they had no other choice if they wanted to survive. And if people accepted without any mitigation the despotic measures and the unprecedented constraints to which they have been subjected, this was not just because they dreaded the pandemic but, presumably, because they also knew more or less unwittingly that the world in which they had lived up until then could not continue to exist—it was too unjust and too inhumane. Needless to say, governments are preparing an even more inhumane and unjust world; but in any case, and on both sides, it was in a way foretold that the previous world—as we are now starting to call it—could not continue to exist. There is surely in this, as in any foreboding, a religious element. Health has replaced salvation, biological life has taken the place of eternal life, and the Church, which has been accustomed for quite some time to compromising with mundane exigencies, has more or less explicitly consented to this substitution. We do not regret the ending of this world. We have no nostalgia for the notions of the human and of the divine that the implacable waves of time are erasing from the shore of history. But we reject with equal conviction the mute and faceless bare life and the health religion that governments are proposing. We are not awaiting either a new god or a new human being. We rather seek, here and now, among the ruins around us, a humbler, simpler form of life. We know that such a life is not a mirage, because we have memories and experiences of it—even if, inside and outside of ourselves, opposing forces are always pushing it back into oblivion.

"Argumentum e silentio." Speak loudly now, unspoken word.

Notes

1   "Fracta nave de mercibus disputo."

2   Walter Benjamin, "Goethe's Elective Affinities", trans. Stanley Corngold, in *Selected Writings*, i: *1913–1926*, ed. Marcus Bullock and Michael W. Jennings (Cambridge: Belknap Press, 1996), 356.

3   Michel de Montaigne, in *Selected Essays*, trans. James B. Atkinson and David Sices (Indianapolis: Hackett Publishing Company, 2012), 17.

4   Elias Canetti, *Crowds and Power*, trans. Carol Stewart (New York: Viking Press, 1963), 15–6.

5   Ibid. 34.

6   Ibid. 55.

7   Thucydides, *The Peloponnesian War*, trans. Martin Hammond (Oxford University Press, 2009), 99.

8   [*Translator's note.* This sentence appears as the epigraph to Giorgio Agamben, *State of Exception*, trans. Kevin Attell (Chicago: The University of Chicago Press, 2005), ix.]

9   See n. 3.

10   This article follows and elaborates on the text of an interview

published in the newspaper *La Verità* on 21 April 2020.

[11] 1 Thessalonians 5:17.

[12] [*Translator's note*. The author uses the expression 'worst case scenario' in the original Italian text.]

[13] [*Translator's note*. Both 'health safety' and 'biosecurity' (here in parentheses) are in English in the original.]

[14] Hannah Arendt, "We Refugees", *Menorah Journal*, 31/1 (January 1943), 69–77.

[15] Yan Thomas, "Citoyens et résidents dans les cités de l'Empire romain. Essai sur le droit d'origine", in *Identité et droit de l'autre*, ed. Laurent Mayali (Berkeley: University of California at Berkeley, 1994), 54.

[16] Karl Binding and Alfred Hoche, *Allowing the Destruction of Life Unworthy of Life: Its Measure and Form*, trans. Cristina Modak (Suzeteo Enterprises, n.p., 2015).

[17] Carl Schmitt, *Political Theology: Four Chapters on the Concept of Sovereignty*, trans. George Schwab (Chicago: University of Chicago Press, 2005), 5.

[18] Marcus Tullius Cicero, *On the Republic and On the Laws*, trans. David Fott (Ithaca: Cornell University Press, 2014), 139.

[19] Martin Heidegger, *Being and Time*, trans. Joan Stambaugh and Dennis J. Schmidt (Albany: State University of New York Press, 2010), 133.

[20] Ibid.

[21] Ibid. 131.

[22] Ibid.

[23] Ibid. 133.

[24] Ibid.

[25] Ibid. 136.

[26] Ibid. 136–7.

[27] Benedictus de Spinoza, *Spinoza's Ethics*, ed. Clare Carlisle and trans. George Eliot (Princeton: Princeton University Press, 2020), 178.

28 Heidegger, *Being and Time*, 137.
29 Ibid.
30 Ibid.
31 Ibid. 138.
32 Ibid.
33 Ibid. 180.
34 Ibid.
35 Ibid. [*Translator's note.* Heidegger uses the English term 'relevant' in the original text.]
36 Ibid. 181.
37 Ibid. 183.
38 Ibid. 137.

GIORGIO AGAMBEN is a philosopher and political theorist who has been described as "one of the most vital and most discussed figures in academia". Renowned for his insights into the history and contemporary crises of Western thought, his many works include *The End of the Poem* (Stanford University Press), *Infancy and History* (Verso Books), *State of Exception* (The University of Chicago Press), and *The Use of Bodies* (Stanford University Press), the latter of which brought to a conclusion his nine-volume *Homo Sacer* series. Currently based in Italy, he has held a number of distinguished academic posts, including the Baruch Spinoza Chair at the European Graduate School.

Made in the USA
Las Vegas, NV
21 December 2021

39141428R00059